Kids in the Garden!

Let's Get Growing!

Gardening is fun! Here are some things you need to know before you begin.

Growing Places

You don't need a garden to grow things. Everything in this book will grow in containers on:

- roof terraces
- windowledges
- balconies
- windowboxes
- yards and patios
- paths and steps

Garden Safety

- Always get help from a grown-up, especially when you see this sign.
- Wear gardening gloves, especially if you have a cut on your hand.
- Wash your hands carefully after gardening.
- If you get liquid plant food on your skin, wash it off right away.
- Gardens can be messy places. Wear old clothes and shoes, like wellies!

Equipment

Here are some things you need:

- compost
- clingfilm
- fork
- seed trays
- canes or sticks
- growing-bag
- stones or pebbles
- garden twine
- gardening gloves
- plastic bags
- trowel
- kneeling mat

Containers

- Flowerpots are made of pot or plastic. Put drip trays or saucers under them.
- Hanging baskets come in metal or plastic. Use them with liners.

Recycle   Instead of buying flowerpots, recycle containers:

- fromage frais and yogurt pots
- fruit and vegetable trays
- plastic buckets
- wooden boxes
- washing up bowls
- wastebins
- baskets
- margarine or butter tubs
- egg boxes

⚠ Wash them before use and ask a grown-up to make holes in the bottom.

How Plants Grow   Plants need two things to grow:

1. LIGHT

- Plants use energy from the sun to make their own food. Without sunlight they will die.

2. WATER

- Use a watering can to water big plants. Use a mister for seedlings and little plants.
- Water little and often, especially if it's hot. Keep the soil or compost damp, not wet.
- A layer of gravel or pebbles in containers drains water away so roots don't get too wet.
- Keep a big stone on soil or compost. Check it every day. If the stone is damp, don't water. If the stone is dry, water.

Lists and Labels

- Make a list of what you grow, or draw a plan.
- Tick the plants that grow well. Cross the ones that don't.
- Push labels into soil or compost. Use a waterproof pen or a pencil. Write: • plant name   • colour   • date planted
- Buy labels, or recycle washed flat lolly sticks.

Friends and Enemies

Get to know plant friends – and enemies!

- ladybirds
- bees
- worms
- butterflies

🙂

- slugs
- snails
- greenfly
- caterpillars

🙁

And last of all ...have fun!

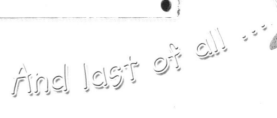

Tasty Tomatoes

Little cherry tomatoes are quick and easy to grow, and good to eat!

To grow 3 you need:

- 3 small flowerpots about 7cm across (or 3 washed yogurt pots)
- 3 large flowerpots about 25cm across (or 3 buckets)
- pebbles or stones
- multi-purpose compost
- cherry tomato seeds
- liquid tomato food

1.

Fill 3 little pots with compost. Push a seed into each pot so that it is just under the compost. Water.

2.

Put the pots somewhere light (like a windowledge). Check them every day and keep the compost moist. In about 4 weeks they will grow into little plants.

3.

This is the time to move them to the bigger pots. Put a layer of pebbles in the base and fill with compost to 10cm from the top.

4.

Tip each little pot and its plant upside down and ease out, compost and all, as on page 12. Put each plant into a big pot and fill in the gaps with compost. Press down gently but firmly, and water.

5.

Feed with liquid tomato food. The pack will tell you how much to use and how often to feed. Check the plants every day and water when they need it.

6.

When your tomato plants have little yellow flowers you can put them outside in a sunny place, out of the wind. When each flower dies a baby tomato will grow in its place.

Keep feeding and watering, and your tomatoes will swell, and turn from green – to orange – to bright red. This means they are ripe, so pick – and eat!

Grow large tomatoes in the same way. They are bigger plants, so grow them in deep buckets or growing-bags. Tie the stalks to garden canes, as on page 11.

Tomatoes come in different shapes, sizes and colours. Large tomatoes grow on tall plants. Small, sweet ones grow on small plants.

Not all tomatoes grow at the same time of the year. Some grow indoors, some outside. Read the packet carefully.

Collect your own seeds. Cut open a tomato and scoop out the pips. Dry on kitchen paper, then plant as above.

Grow 3 tiny 'tumbling' or 'bush' tomato plants in a hanging basket.

Buy little ready-grown plants. Feed and water them and move to bigger containers as they grow.

Sunflowers ... Suns-on-stalks

Sunflowers got their name because they look like yellow suns. They can grow as tall as you in weeks!

Tiny seeds like these ... grow into big, tall sunflowers!

You need:

- sunflower seeds
- an egg box
- multi-purpose compost
- plant mister
- large plantpots or plastic buckets
- garden canes or sticks
- garden twine

1.

Fill a plastic egg box with compost and press a seed into each hole. Or use a cardboard egg box and cover with a clear plastic tray or loose clingfilm.

2.

Add water to make the compost damp. Close the lid and put the carton where there is lots of light, like a windowledge.

3.

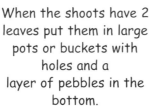

Use a water mister to keep the compost damp. In about a week tiny shoots will push up through the compost.

4.

When the shoots have 2 leaves put them in large pots or buckets with holes and a layer of pebbles in the bottom.

5.

Keep the compost damp. When the seedlings grow taller push canes into the pots and tie to the stalks using soft twine.

6.

When it's warm move the plants outside in their pots, or plant in the ground. Tie the stalks to the sticks again as they grow taller.

 Buy packets of seeds from garden centres and supermarkets. Read what it says on the packet and choose the size or colour you like best. The packet will tell you when to plant them.

 Use washed yogurt pots or vegetable trays for seeds. Use plastic buckets as large plantpots. Get a grown-up to make holes in the bottom so water can drain out. Why not paint your pots?

See who can grow the tallest sunflower. Some can grow to 3 metres! Write your name and the date you planted your seeds on a plant label. Make a chart and write down the date and height. You'll be amazed how fast they grow!

 Keep the compost damp. Check it every day, especially if it's hot. Use a plant mister to water tiny seedlings and a watering can for larger plants.

After the sunflower dies and dries out, collect the seeds to plant next year. Keep them in a paper bag or envelope.

Baskets and Boxes

Make instant displays using ready-grown plants from a nursery or garden centre.

For a hanging pot you need:

- plastic hanging pot
- pebbles or stones
- multi-purpose compost
- trailing plant (one with stems that grow downwards)

1.

Put a layer of pebbles or stones in the base of the basket. Half fill with compost.

2.

Tip the plant out of its pot. Do this very carefully! Put your fingers on either side of the plant stem. Tip the pot upside down and catch the plant and compost as it slips out.

3.

Sit the plant in the middle of the basket. Fill in the space around it with more compost. Press down gently but firmly, and water.

4.

Ask a grown-up to fix a hook for your hanging pot. Put it where there is good light, and keep it watered. It can go outside if it is warm and there is no frost.

For a box of plants you need:

- rectangular plastic box or planter
- pebbles or stones
- multi-purpose compost
- tray or pack of plants (at least 6)

1.

Put a layer of pebbles or stones in the base of the box. Fill with compost.

2.

Using a trowel, make a little hole for each plant. Space them out evenly.

3.

Tip the plants out of their pack or tray, as on page 12, and put one in each hole.

4.

Use your fingers to fill in the holes with compost. Press firmly, and water.

Use one kind of plant, or a mixture of different ones. Plant the tallest at the back, and smaller ones at the front.

Add a few seeds of quick-growing trailing plants like nasturtiums to hanging pots.

If you plant up a wire hanging basket, add a liner to help keep the compost damp.

Put plant food sticks or pellets in your containers.

Trays of little plants, or tiny 'plugs' are much cheaper than bigger plants. Look after them, and they will soon grow.

13

Lettuces and Salad Leaves

Lettuces and salad leaves grow very quickly.
Some will be ready to eat in just a few weeks!

You need:

- seed tray, at least 10cm deep
- drip tray
- multi-purpose compost
- packet of mixed lettuce or salad leaf seeds

1.

Put the seed tray on a drip tray. Fill with compost, and water so that it is damp.

2.

Sprinkle about 10 seeds in one strip of the tray. Each seed will grow into a plant so don't plant too many at once. Cover with a very thin layer of compost.

3.

Put the seed tray somewhere warm and light. Keep the compost moist, adding water to the drip tray.

4.

A week later, sow a few more seeds in another strip of the tray. Sow strip 3 a week later. This way, your lettuces won't all be ready at the same time!

5.

Seedlings will start to grow after about 2 weeks. If they are crowded, gently pull out 1 or 2 to make space for the others.

6.

Water every day. In about 8 to 12 weeks the lettuces will be big enough to eat!

 When you pull out a lettuce to eat, plant 1 or 2 seeds in its place.

 You can move the little plants outside if it's warm enough. Don't put them in very hot sun, or they will die.

  To grow lots of salad leaves, use a growing-bag, sowing seeds in strips, as above. Start off indoors then move outside. Ask a grown-up to cut the plastic.

 Lettuces like mizuna and oak leaf are called 'cut and come again'. Use scissors to cut off as many leaves as you need, and more will grow in their place!

 Salad leaves come in lots of lovely colours and leaf shapes. Grow some among flowers or herbs.

 Sow a few radish seeds among your lettuces. They will be ready to eat in just 3 to 6 weeks!

 The leaves of some weeds and plants that grow wild are good to eat, like dandelion and chickweed. Grow them from seed, following the instructions on the packet.

Annual Flowers

Grow some annual flowers. They come in lots of shapes and sizes, and in all the colours of the rainbow.

In a few weeks you'll have colourful flowers like these

You need:

- annual seeds; choose flowers that will grow in containers
- multi-purpose compost
- large plantpot or container, about 30cm across
- pebbles or gravel
- plant labels

1.

Put a layer of pebbles or gravel in the container. Fill with compost, and water.

2.

Sprinkle on about 20 or 30 seeds and cover with a very thin layer of compost. Plant one kind of flower, or a mixture. Add labels, as on page 7.

3.

Water gently, using a plant mister. Put in a warm, light place, like a windowledge, and keep the compost damp. In about 2 weeks tiny seedlings will grow.

4.

Later on, if it's warm, and the little plants are growing well, you can put them outside. Choose a sunny place out of the wind. Check every day and keep them watered.

All About Annuals

Annuals grow and
die in one year:

grow from seed

flower

die

make seed

Annual seeds
are amazing!

A tiny poppy
seed this size

will grow into

... this!

Choose annual seeds
carefully: Some

• will grow in containers and
  windowboxes
• trail from hanging baskets
• can be sown straight into
  open ground
• need to be started off
  indoors

Plant a packet of
mixed annual seeds.
These are fun
because you don't
know what will grow
... until it grows!

Pinch off dead
flower heads, and
cut flowers for
vases. More will
soon grow.

As annuals die they make
seeds. Collect them, dry
on kitchen paper and put
in an envelope. Label and
plant next year. Some
annuals 'self-seed'.
Their seeds fall into the
soil and will grow
next year.

Seed Packets

tell you all you need to know.

The front tells you:

what the flower looks like

its common name, eg poppy,
and Latin name, papaver

how many seeds are inside

The back tells you:

how tall and wide the flower will grow

when and where to plant the seeds

how long the seeds will take to grow

when the plant will flower

if the flower is easy or difficult
to grow

Squashes and Pumpkins

Growing these vegetables is fun because they grow very large very quickly!

The squash family of vegetables includes marrows, courgettes and pumpkins. Some are the size of a little apple, others are huge and fat!

You need:

- 3 pots or containers, about 5cm across
- fine gravel
- multi-purpose compost
- squash seeds; choose 'dwarf' or 'bush' kinds
- clingfilm
- 3 pots or containers about 10cm across
- 3 pots or containers about 15cm across
- 1 growing-bag
- liquid plant food for vegetables

1.

Put a thin layer of fine gravel in the bottom of 3 small containers. Fill with compost and push a seed into each so that it is 1cm deep, with its tip upwards. Water.

2.

Cover with clingfilm to make mini greenhouses for the seeds. Put in a warm place where there is plenty of sunlight, like a windowledge or conservatory.

3.

After 2 or 3 weeks little seedlings will appear. Take off the clingfilm and when the seedlings have at least 2 leaves move them to 10cm pots. Do this carefully, as on page 12.

4.

Keep the compost damp, but not wet. When more leaves grow, then hairy flower stalks, move to bigger pots, about 15cm across.

5.

Ask a grown-up to cut three holes in the growing-bag. When the plants are bigger, put a plant in each hole and water. They can go outside if it's warm, but not in very strong sun or windy places. If you have a garden, plant the squashes in open ground.

6.

Yellow flowers will appear, then fruits will grow. The squashes are working hard, so add liquid vegetable food when you water them, and pick the fruits often when they are ready – more will soon grow.

Other Vegetables

Try growing other vegetables, like peas and beans. Choose seeds that grow fast and are suitable for containers if you don't have a garden.

Squashes with huge leaves need lots of space! Choose ones that will grow in the space you have.

To grow extra-large squashes, mix animal manure into the growing-bag compost. Use 1 part manure to 3 parts compost.

Squashes and pumpkins are good to eat. Try them roasted, and in stews or soups.

Watch out for slugs! They love eating young plants.

If you don't have space for a big growing-bag, grow a small 'patio' squash in a bucket.

Squashes need a lot of water, so check them every day, especially in hot, dry weather.

Grow big pumpkins to make jack o' lanterns for Halloween. Ask a grown-up to cut off the top, scoop out the flesh and make holes for eyes, nose and mouth. Put a nightlight inside to make a spooky face!

Colourful Bulbs

Some plants grow from bulbs. Different ones flower at different times of the year. Their labels will tell you when and how deep to plant them.

You need:

- large pot, windowbox or container at least 25cm deep
- pebbles or stones
- multi-purpose compost
- bag of daffodil or narcissus bulbs
- plant label

1.

Put a layer of pebbles in the container and half fill with compost.

2.

Press some bulbs gently into the compost, pointed ends up. Read the packaging for how much space you need to leave between them. Cover with a 7 or 8cm layer of compost.

3.

Press another layer of bulbs into the compost. Fill the container with compost to 2cm below the rim. Using your fingers, firm gently, and water.

4.

Add a label as on page 7 and put the pot outside. Keep the compost damp. Soon shoots and leaves will grow, and your bulbs will burst into flower.

Bulbs are sold in bags. Buy ones that are firm and plump, not dried up or soft.

You can plant bulbs in open ground. If you are planting lots, use a bulb planter like this one. It's much easier than digging lots of little holes.

Some bulbs can be left in the ground or in containers from year to year. If you dig them up, keep them somewhere dark, cool and dry until it's time to plant them again.

Different bulbs grow in different places. Read the labels to find ones that grow well where you live.

Some bulbs grow indoors. Labels will tell you which ones, and how to grow them.

Mix and match colours:

- bright reds, yellows and blues
- hot reds and oranges
- cool whites

When you have planted a pot of bulbs, add evergreen ivy and flowering plants to the pot. They will flower while the bulbs are growing.

Make a bulb garden in a large container.

Plant:

tall flowers at the back

medium flowers around them

small flowers at the front